All you need to know about Malta

Copyright © 2023 Jonas Hoffmann-Schmidt and Linda Amber Chambers.

All rights reserved. This book, including all its parts, is protected by copyright. Any use outside the narrow limits of copyright law is prohibited without the written consent of the author. This book has been created using artificial intelligence to provide unique and informative content.

Disclaimer: This book is for entertainment purposes only. The information, facts and views contained therein have been researched and compiled to the best of our knowledge and belief. Nevertheless, the author and the publisher assume no liability for the accuracy or completeness of the information. Readers should consult with professionals before making any decisions based on this information. Use of this book is the responsibility of the reader.

The History of Malta: An Overview 6
The Prehistoric Temples of Malta 8
The Knights of Malta: The Order of St. John
.... 10
The Napoleonic era in Malta 12
Malta under British rule 14
Malta's independence: 1964 to the present. 16
The Maltese flag and coat of arms 18
Malta's unique geography 20
The Maltese Wildlife: From Malta Falcon to
Sea Turtle 22
Malta's culinary diversity: from Pastizzi to
Rabbit Stew 24
Maltese wines and liqueurs: an enjoyable
discovery 26
Valletta: Malta's capital and UNESCO World
Heritage Site 28
The three historic towns: Birgu, Senglea and
Bormla 30
The megalithic temples of Ħaġar Qim and
Mnajdra 32
Gozo: Malta's sister island 34

Comino: The small island of the Blue Lagoon 36

The Blue Grotto: A Natural Wonder Point 38

The fortified city of Mdina: The silent heart of Malta 40

The Maltese folk festivals and celebrations. 42

The tradition of Carnival in Malta 44

The Maltese Music Scene: From Għana to Modern Pop Music..46

The Maltese Art Scene: From Caravaggio to the Present 48

Religion in Malta: From Roman times to the present day..50

Maltese folklore and customs........................52

Maltese craftsmanship and the art of filigree 54

The Maltese Language: Insight into Maltese 56

The School System and Education in Malta 58

Medical care in Malta......................................60

Maltese legal system and justice 62

Malta's Economy: From Tourism to the Financial Industry..64

Maltese Architecture: A Journey Through the Centuries 66

The Maltese Transport System: From Buses to Ferries 68

Outdoor activities: scuba diving, hiking, and more 70

The Maltese Carnival: From Costumes to Parades 72

Nightlife in Malta: bars, clubs and events ... 74

Maltese souvenirs and shopping 76

Naturalization in Malta: Life on the Island ... 78

Maltese hospitality and the culture of hospitality 81

Sustainability and environmental protection in Malta 83

Future outlook: Where is Malta headed? 85

Epilogue 87

The History of Malta: An Overview

Malta's history is as old as it is fascinating, marked by a variety of cultural influences, conquests and historical turning points. The island of Malta, located in the heart of the Mediterranean Sea, is of great importance not only because of its geographical location, but also because of its rich past dating back to the Stone Age.

The earliest settlement in Malta can be dated to around 5200 BC, when the first Neolithic farmers reached the island. These people left behind an amazing legacy in the form of the megalithic temples, some of which are among the oldest free-standing structures in the world. The impressive temples of Ħaġar Qim and Mnajdra are excellent examples of these prehistoric monuments, which are still admired today.

The Phoenicians, a seafaring nation of the ancient Middle East, arrived in Malta in the 8th century BC and established trading posts on the island. Later, Malta became part of the Roman Empire, and the Romans left their mark in the form of architectural remains and Roman villas.

In the 4th century AD, Malta became a bastion of Christianity when the Apostle Paul landed on the island and spread Christianity. The remains of a Roman catacomb complex in Rabat are a testimony to this early Christian community.

Malta's history took a dramatic turn when the Arabs conquered the island in 870, making it an important centre for trade and culture. Under Arab rule, Malta flourished, and many Arab influences, including in architecture and language, can still be felt today.

In 1091, the Normans reconquered the island from the Arabs and founded the Kingdom of Sicily, which included Malta. Later, Malta became an important base for the Order of Malta, a Christian order of chivalry dedicated to defending Christianity. The Order of Malta's reign lasted until 1798, when Napoleon Bonaparte conquered the island and ushered in a brief but formative period of French occupation.

After Napoleon's fall, Malta came under British rule and remained a part of the British Empire until 1964. During this period, Malta developed into an important strategic base and played a crucial role during World War II.

Malta's independence was achieved in 1964, and the island was declared a republic in 1974. Since then, Malta has had a modern history of political developments, economic growth and an increasingly important role in the international context.

This summary of Malta's history illustrates the variety of influences and events that have shaped this fascinating island. From prehistoric temples to recent independence, Malta's history reflects the storied past and unmistakable identity of this remarkable Mediterranean island.

The Prehistoric Temples of Malta

The prehistoric temples of Malta are undoubtedly among the most fascinating archaeological sites in the world. Found on the Maltese islands of Malta, Gozo and Comino, these impressive structures shed a bright light on the distant times of the Neolithic, also known as the Neolithic, and are among the oldest free-standing structures in human history.

The history of these temples dates back to around 5200 BC, when the first Neolithic farmers came to Malta and began to build these monumental structures. One of the most famous temples is Ħaġar Qim, which is located on Malta's main Maltese island. Ħaġar Qim consists of several cleverly arranged temples built from large limestone blocks. The precise construction and the magnificent stone processing are astonishing examples of the craftsmanship of the people of that time.

Another impressive temple complex is Mnajdra, which is located in close proximity to Ħaġar Qim. Mnajdra is characterized by its refined alignments, which are related to the celestial phenomena. The plays of sunlight that occur in the temples during the equinox refer to the remarkable astronomical knowledge and religious rituals of Malta's Neolithic inhabitants.

The temples of Ġgantija on the island of Gozo are also of great importance. This temple complex consists of two temples that are believed to be the oldest free-standing temples in the world. The monumental nature of these temples and the massive stone blocks from which they were built testify to the organizational and technological mastery of the people of that time.

It is important to emphasize that the exact meaning of these temples and the religious or cultural practices associated with them are still the subject of intense research and speculation. It is believed that they were used for religious rituals, cultic purposes, and possibly also for astronomical observations. The statuettes and artifacts found in the temples indicate a complex culture associated with these sites.

The prehistoric temples of Malta are not only testimonies of the past, but also a symbol of the amazing skills and cultural heritage of the Neolithic society that created them. Their preservation and research are invaluable to archaeology and historical research, as they offer us insights into the earliest chapters of human civilization and further enrich Malta's unique history.

The Knights of Malta: The Order of St. John

The history of Malta is inextricably linked to the Order of Saint John of Jerusalem, also known as the Knights of St. John. This order of chivalry, whose origins date back to the 11th century, played a crucial role in the development of Malta and shaped the islands for centuries.

The Order of Saint John was founded during the Crusades to ensure the care and care of pilgrims in the Holy Land. Originally a monastic brotherhood, the order quickly developed into a powerful military organization. He was given the nickname "Knights of St. John" because of his headquarters in Jerusalem.

After the expulsion of Christians from the Holy Land in the 13th century, the Order established its new home on the island of Rhodes. There he flourished and established an impressive fortress that withstood the attacks of various powers. The Knights of St. John were known for their bravery in the fight against the Ottoman troops and their devotion to the care of the sick.

In 1530, Charles V, Emperor of the Holy Roman Empire, granted the Knights of St. John the island of Malta as a fief. This step marked the beginning of a new era in the history of Malta and the Order. The Knights of St. John took over the fortress of Birgu (Vittoriosa), expanded it further and named it Fort St. Angelo. This fortress and the surrounding towns, including Valletta, became impregnable bulwarks of Christianity.

During the Siege of Malta in 1565, considered one of the most famous sieges in history, the Knights heroically resisted the attacks of the Ottomans under Suleiman the Magnificent. Their steadfastness and determination earned them worldwide recognition and respect. The Battle of Malta, as we know it today, ended with the retreat of the Ottomans and strengthened the Order's position in the Mediterranean.

The Knights of Malta lived by a strict code of conduct and were dedicated to defending Christianity, caring for the sick and assisting those in need. Its emblem, the eight-pointed Maltese Cross, is known worldwide and is a symbol of charity and bravery.

Over the centuries, the political landscape changed, and the Order's power gradually waned. In 1798, Malta was conquered by Napoleon Bonaparte, and the Knights of St. John were expelled from the island. Nevertheless, the Order survived and eventually found a new home in Rome, where it continues to carry out humanitarian work as the Sovereign Order of Malta.

The story of the Knights of Malta is a fascinating chapter in the history of Malta. Its heritage, architecture and influence on Malta's culture are still visible today, reminding us of a time when the island was a bastion of Christianity and chivalry.

The Napoleonic era in Malta

The Napoleonic era in Malta marks a crucial period in the island's history, marked by conquest, political upheaval and a brief but significant interlude under French rule. This chapter of Malta's history dates back to the years 1798 to 1800 and left deep traces on the island.

In 1798, during the Napoleonic Wars, Napoleon Bonaparte conquered the island of Malta from the Knights of Saint John, who had previously ruled over Malta. The Knights of St. John, also known as the Order of Malta, were a powerful religious and military organization that had been based in Malta since the 16th century. Their expulsion and the French conquest marked the end of their rule on the island.

Napoleon planned to use Malta as a strategic base for his military operations in the Mediterranean. However, the French occupation brought about significant political, economic and social changes. The power of the church was curtailed, feudal structures abolished and political reforms introduced. The French Revolution had an impact on these developments and influenced the political landscape of Malta.

During his brief reign in Malta, Napoleon also established the "Institut national", an educational institution designed to help promote education on the island. This institute had a lasting impact on Malta's education system, contributing to the dissemination of knowledge and ideas.

Despite some reforms, French rule encountered resistance and unrest from the Maltese population. The Maltese felt alienated from the French and longed for a return to religious stability and the old traditions of the Order of Malta.

In 1800, Malta was finally conquered by the British, who controlled the island in the following years and who welcomed the Maltese people. This marked the end of the Napoleonic era in Malta.

The Napoleonic era in Malta was a time of change and uncertainty. However, it left a lasting mark on Maltese history, both in terms of political changes and in terms of education and culture. This chapter of history illustrates Malta's complex relationship with the European powers during the Napoleonic era and the impact of this period on the island and its inhabitants.

Malta under British rule

The era of British rule in Malta spanned almost 160 years and shaped the island's history and development in many ways. This period officially began in 1814 and did not end until 1964, when Malta gained its independence from Great Britain.

The British took over Malta as part of the Treaty of Paris of 1814, which marked the starting point for their long presence on the island. Malta became an important strategic base of the British Empire in the Mediterranean. The island's well-protected natural harbors, including the Grand Harbor, proved to be crucial naval and commercial bases.

During British rule, Malta experienced a period of economic boom. The British invested in the island's infrastructure, including roads, ports, and railways, and promoted trade and shipping. This led to a certain period of economic prosperity, especially in the areas of trade and shipbuilding.

The British administration also introduced political and social reforms. The Constitution of 1849, known as the "Maltese Constitution", granted the Maltese some self-government and political rights. This contributed to the development of a rising political class and paved the way for further political reforms in the future.

During the First World War, Malta played an important role as a supply base for the Allies and as a naval hospital. This helped to further strengthen the British presence on the island.

The period of the Second World War was particularly drastic for Malta. The island suffered heavy bombardment by the Axis powers and became the "Siege of Malta". The valiant defence of the Maltese and the determination of the British forces led to Malta being awarded the George Cross Medal for its heroic resistance.

After the Second World War, a political movement for more independence began. In 1964, Malta finally gained sovereignty and became independent from Great Britain, but remained a member of the Commonwealth. This marked the end of the long era of British rule in Malta.

The period of British rule in Malta was a complex period that brought political, economic and social changes. She left behind a cultural legacy that can still be felt in Maltese society today. The relationship between Malta and Great Britain is close and historically rooted, and British rule has been instrumental in Malta's modern history.

Malta's independence: 1964 to the present

The period from Malta's independence in 1964 to the present day has been marked by continuous development and change. This chapter of Malta's history reflects the path of a country that gained its sovereignty and evolved into a modern, independent state.

On September 21, 1964, Malta officially became independent from Great Britain and entered the ranks of independent nations. The country became a member of the Commonwealth of Nations and began to shape its own political and economic paths. Sir Anthony Mamo became Malta's first president, and George Borg Olivier became the country's first prime minister.

The years after independence brought political changes. In 1971, Dom Mintoff was elected Prime Minister and introduced socialist policies that strained relations with Britain. This led to the closure of the British military bases in Malta in 1979. The political landscape was marked by political instability and controversial political decisions.

Malta joined the European Union in 1974 and began to reap the economic and political benefits of EU membership. Integration into the European Union was an important milestone in Malta's history, helping to strengthen the country's economy and improve the quality of life of its citizens.

The 1980s were marked by political polarization and tensions between the two political parties, the Partit Nazzjonalista (Nationalist Party) and the Partit Laburista

(Workers' Party). The political landscape remained turbulent, and governments changed frequently.

In the 1990s, Malta experienced a period of political stability and economic reforms under the government of Prime Minister Eddie Fenech Adami. The country increased its focus on the tourism, service sector, and shipping, which led to sustained economic growth.

Malta joined the European Union in 2004 and adopted the euro as its currency. This cemented Malta's integration into the EU and strengthened its position as a major player in the region.

However, Malta's recent history has also been marked by political scandals and challenges. A highlight was the murder of journalist Daphne Caruana Galizia in 2017, which attracted international attention and raised questions about press freedom and the fight against corruption in Malta.

Today, Malta is a modern European state with a thriving economy, a stable political landscape, and a diverse society. The island nation has become a popular tourist destination, attracting visitors from all over the world. Malta's history since independence reflects the ups and downs, the challenges and successes of a small country that has found its place in the world and continues to shape its identity.

The Maltese flag and coat of arms

The Maltese flag and coat of arms are not only symbols of the country, but also carry a rich historical significance and tell the story of Malta in a visual way. The Maltese flag is made up of the colours red and white and is a distinctive feature of the Maltese identity and national pride.

The flag of Malta, also known as the "George Cross", stands out for its eye-catching design. It consists of a vertical band divided into two parts in the middle, with the upper part being red and the lower part white. In the upper left corner of the red field is the George Cross, a white cross on a red background. This cross is a symbol of the courage and bravery of the Maltese during the Second World War and was awarded to Malta by King George VI.

The flag of Malta has its roots in the long history of the island and its various rulers. The colours red and white have traditionally been associated with Malta and date back to the time of the Order of Malta, which ruled the island in the Middle Ages. The George Cross, emblazoned on the flag, commemorates the heroic defence of Malta during the siege of 1940-1942, when the island was bombed by the Axis powers.

The Maltese coat of arms is another significant national symbol. It depicts a shield divided into four fields. In the two upper panels, a golden lion on a red background and a silver three-pointed tower on a red background can be seen. The lower two panels depict a silver St. Andrew's cross on a red background and a golden stag on a red background.

The Maltese coat of arms has a complex history, dating back to different phases of Maltese history and the influences of different rulers. The lions represent Malta's historical ties to kingdoms such as Sicily and Aragon. The three-pointed towers represent the fortified cities of Malta, which played an important role in the defense of the island. The St. Andrew's cross commemorates Malta's connection to the Order of St. John, while the golden stag may indicate the connection to the Hohenstaufen family.

Together, the Maltese flag and coat of arms form a powerful symbol of the Maltese nation and its history. They commemorate the bravery and resistance of the Maltese in difficult times, while also representing the cultural and historical diversity of the island. These symbols are more than just graphic representations; they are an expression of the pride and identity of a country that carries its history with dignity and pride.

Malta's unique geography

The geography of Malta is as unique as it is fascinating, and has shaped the history, culture and character of the islands for thousands of years. This small archipelago in the heart of the Mediterranean Sea is characterized by a multitude of geological features that make it a unique and remarkable place.

Malta consists of three main islands: Malta, Gozo and Comino, as well as some smaller, uninhabited islands. The islands are located about 80 kilometers south of Sicily and are surrounded by crystal clear, azure waters. This Mediterranean paradise has shaped a maritime culture and history that is deeply woven into the consciousness of the Maltese people.

One of Malta's most striking geological features is the limestone cliffs that dominate the islands. These rocks are the result of millions of years of geological activity and erosion. The characteristic yellowish-white colouring of the limestone gives Malta its unmistakable appearance and is an important part of the architecture and road construction on the island.

Malta's coastline is characterised by numerous bays, cliffs and caves, perfect for exploring by boat or swimming. One of the most famous coastal formations is the "Blue Grotto" on the southwest coast of Malta, which is known for its crystal clear waters and impressive caves.

The island of Gozo, located just a short ferry ride from Malta, offers stunning scenery, including rolling hills, fertile valleys and picturesque coastlines. The Gozo 'Azure Window', a natural stone arch, was a well-known landmark until it collapsed during a storm in 2017.

Another notable geographical feature of Malta is the absence of rivers and lakes. The islands have a semi-arid climate characterized by limited rainfall. The lack of natural freshwater sources has forced the Maltese to skillfully collect rainwater and create artificial water reservoirs.

Malta's unique geography has also shaped its agriculture and land use. Terraced fields, stone walls and drywall are typical of the Maltese landscape and serve to take advantage of the limited fertile soil.

Malta's location in the Mediterranean Sea has made the islands an important hub for trade and shipping. The natural harbour of Valletta, one of the deepest and safest harbours in the Mediterranean, played a crucial role in Malta's history and contributed to the island's strategic importance.

Malta's unique geography, from the limestone cliffs to the picturesque coastline and fertile valleys, gives the archipelago its distinctive character and has made it a sought-after tourist destination. This geography has shaped the culture, history and daily life of the Maltese people and remains an integral part of Malta's identity.

The Maltese Wildlife: From Malta Falcon to Sea Turtle

Malta's wildlife is diverse and shaped by the islands' unique geographical location in the Mediterranean Sea. This diversity encompasses a wide range of habitats, from the coast to the rocky hills and valleys that make up the Maltese landscape.

A notable animal closely associated with Malta is the Malta falcon (Falco melitensis). This rare bird of prey is endemic to the Maltese islands and is considered one of the rarest birds in the world. With its impressive appearance and majestic flying skills, the Malta Falcon is a symbol of Malta's wildlife and an important part of the island's natural heritage.

Malta's wildlife also includes a wide variety of marine life. The waters around Malta are known for their biodiversity and provide habitat for fish, dolphins, whales and sea turtles. One of the most notable species is the loggerhead sea turtle (Caretta caretta), which breeds in Maltese waters and can also be found as a guest in the shallow bays and caves of the islands.

The Maltese coast and its bays provide habitat for an abundance of marine organisms, including numerous species of fish, crustaceans and molluscs. The diversity of the marine life makes Malta a popular destination for divers and snorkelers who want to explore the colorful coral reefs and abundant marine wildlife.

Malta's rocky hills and valleys are home to various species of reptiles and insects. The Maltese wall lizard (Podarcis filfolensis) is an endemic species of lizard that has adapted well to the dry living conditions on the island. Several species of butterflies, including the Maltese swallowtail (Papilio machaon melitensis), are also present in the Maltese wildlife.

Malta's birdlife is also abundant and includes migratory birds that visit the islands on their migrations through the Mediterranean. The Maltese cliffs and cliffs provide breeding grounds for various species of seabirds, including gulls and shearwaters.

However, it is important to note that Malta's wildlife also faces challenges and threats. Habitat loss due to human development, illegal hunting, and pollution are some of the issues affecting Malta's wildlife. However, organizations and conservationists are actively engaged in the protection and conservation of native animal species and their habitats.

Maltese wildlife is an integral part of the islands and their unique environment. The preservation of these species and their habitat is vital to preserve Malta's biodiversity and preserve the beauty and uniqueness of Malta's wildlife for future generations.

Malta's culinary diversity: from Pastizzi to Rabbit Stew

Maltese cuisine is as diverse and unique as the history and culture of the islands themselves. From traditional dishes to modern culinary influences, Malta offers a wealth of taste experiences that make the culinary journey through the country a real treat.

A characteristic and popular Maltese dish is the pastizzi. These small pastries covered in puff pastry are available with different fillings, with those filled with ricotta cheese or pea puree being among the best known. Pastizzi are a delicious and inexpensive option for a quick breakfast or snack and are often enjoyed by locals and tourists alike.

Another culinary highlight of Malta is the famous Rabbit Stew (Hasi il-Forn). Rabbit meat is a popular ingredient in Maltese cuisine and is often cooked in a spicy Dutch oven. The meat is slow-cooked and seasoned with garlic, wine, tomatoes and spices, which gives the dish its characteristic flavor. The Rabbit Stew is a traditional Sunday meal and a culinary must-visit for visitors to Malta.

Malta is also known for its fresh seafood. The islands' location in the Mediterranean Sea offers ample opportunity for fresh catches, including fish such as dolphinfish, tuna and swordfish. A popular Maltese fish speciality is lampuki, a spicy fish that is often cooked in a tomato and caper sauce.

Another culinary tradition of Malta is the festive meals during the holidays. During Christmas and Easter, special dishes such as the famous Maltese Christmas Log (Qagħaq tal-Għasel) and the sweet Easter tarts (Figolli) are an indispensable part of the festivities. These treats are ornately decorated and reflect the festive atmosphere of the holidays.

Maltese cuisine has also incorporated Oriental and Italian influences, resulting in a unique fusion of aromas and flavours. An example of this is the popular Maltese soup, Soppa tal-Armla, which refers to the influence of Arabic cuisine and is often made with lentils, vegetables and spices.

In addition to the savoury dishes, Malta also offers a rich selection of desserts. The traditional Maltese dessert Helwa tat-Tork (Turkish Honey) is a sweet made from sesame seeds and sugar, often enjoyed in small, cube-shaped pieces. Another sweet temptation is kannoli, an Italian pastry filled with a creamy ricotta filling.

Malta's culinary diversity reflects the islands' rich history and cultural diversity. The combination of traditional recipes and modern influences makes Maltese cuisine a fascinating aspect of Maltese culture, offering visitors the opportunity to discover and enjoy the flavours and delights of this unique archipelago.

Maltese wines and liqueurs: an enjoyable discovery

The Maltese wines and liqueurs are a real treasure that deserves to be discovered and appreciated. The long history of viticulture in the Maltese Islands dates back to ancient times, and the variety of wines and liqueurs produced here reflects the region's unique climatic conditions and traditions.

Maltese wine production is mainly concentrated on the main island of Malta and its sister island of Gozo. The Mediterranean climate with warm, sunny days and mild nights, combined with the calcareous soils, creates ideal conditions for viticulture. Maltese winemakers have grown a variety of grape varieties, including local varieties such as Gellewża and Girgentina, as well as international varieties such as Cabernet Sauvignon, Merlot, and Chardonnay.

One of the most famous and popular Maltese wines is the "Dingli Cliffs." This dry white wine, made from the Girgentina grape, is characterized by fresh citrus aromas and a lively acidity. It is an excellent accompaniment to seafood and fish dishes and is often enjoyed by locals and tourists.

Another notable Maltese wine is the "Marsala," a sweet dessert wine that is often served after a meal. This aromatic wine, made from the grapes of the Gellewża grape, offers notes of dried fruits, caramel and honey and is a real treat for gourmets.

Malta is also known for its liqueurs, including the famous "Bajtra," a liqueur made from the fruits of the gorse tree. The Bajtra liqueur has a sweet, fruity taste and is often served as a digestif. It is a traditional Maltese drink and a popular souvenir for visitors.

Another Maltese liqueur that is gaining traction is the "Mistra." This herbal liqueur is made from a mixture of herbs, spices and citrus fruits and has a pleasant, slightly bitter taste. Mistra is often drunk as an aperitif and is an integral part of Maltese food culture.

Maltese wines and liqueurs are not only luxury foods, but also an expression of Maltese culture and tradition. Malta's winemakers and distilleries are committed to nurturing and developing this rich heritage, helping to promote Maltese gastronomy and wine traditions.

For visitors to Malta, wine tasting and tours of the wineries and distilleries offer a great opportunity to explore the fascinating world of Maltese wines and liqueurs. The discovery and enjoyment of these local specialties is an enrichment for anyone who wants to experience the culinary diversity and culture of Malta.

Valletta: Malta's capital and UNESCO World Heritage Site

Valletta, the capital of Malta, is undoubtedly one of the most fascinating and historic cities in the Mediterranean. Perched on a peninsula on Malta's northeast coast, this small but impressive town is a true gem of history and culture. Since 1980, Valletta has even been part of the UNESCO World Heritage Site, highlighting its importance and beauty.

Valletta's history dates back to the mid-16th century, when the Order of Malta, also known as the Order of Saint John, founded the city. Construction of the city began in 1566, and Italian architect Francesco Laparelli played a key role in the planning and design of Valletta. The city was named after Jean Parisot de la Valette, the Grand Master of the Order of Malta, who successfully defended the islands against the siege of the Ottomans.

Valletta's architecture is characterised by an impressive ensemble of fortifications, palaces, churches and squares. The ramparts that surround the city bear witness to its strategic importance in Malta's history. The city was designed to provide the best protection against attacks while allowing for efficient defense.

One of Valletta's most recognizable landmarks is the Grand Master's Palace, also known as the Presidential Palace. This impressive palace served as the residence of the Grand Master of the Order of Malta and is now home to the Parliament of Malta and the President's Office. The palace's magnificent rooms are richly decorated and house an impressive collection of artwork and historical artifacts.

St. John's Co-Cathedral is another significant religious site in Valletta. It is a masterpiece of baroque style and impresses visitors with its magnificent façade and stunning interior. The cathedral is also home to the famous painting "The Beheading of John the Baptist" by Caravaggio.

The streets and alleys of Valletta are lined with historic buildings, including numerous palaces that once housed the nobility and knights of the Order of Malta. A reflection of Malta's rich history and culture, these buildings tell tales of chivalry and bravery.

However, Valletta is not only a museum of the past, but also a vibrant city inhabited and used by people. The city is home to a vibrant community of locals and is a hub for arts, culture, and entertainment. Visitors can stroll through the narrow streets, visit traditional Maltese restaurants, experience the hustle and bustle of the squares and enjoy the Maltese hospitality.

Valletta, Malta's capital and UNESCO World Heritage Site, is a place of historical significance and timeless beauty. A living testament to Malta's rich history and culture, it is a place that fascinates and inspires visitors from all over the world. Its heritage is carefully preserved and nurtured to ensure that the history and splendor of this extraordinary city is preserved for future generations.

The three historic towns: Birgu, Senglea and Bormla

The Maltese towns of Birgu, Senglea and Bormla, also known as Cospicua, are three historical gems closely linked to the history of the Order of Malta and the defence of Malta. These cities, together with Valletta, form the so-called "Three Cities" and are an important part of the islands' cultural heritage.

Birgu, also known as Vittoriosa, is one of Malta's oldest and most picturesque towns. It was founded in the Middle Ages and was the capital of Malta for a long time before being replaced by Valletta. The city walls of Birgu are impressive and testify to their strategic importance in Malta's history. Visitors can explore the fortifications that surround the harbor and immerse themselves in history. A notable sight in Birgu is Fort St. Angelo, a powerful defensive work that served various purposes over the centuries and played an important role in Malta's defense.

Senglea, also known as Isla, is located on a small peninsula opposite Valletta and offers stunning views of the capital. The city is known for its narrow streets, historic buildings and fortified bastions. One of the most notable buildings in Senglea is the Basilica of Our Lady of Victories (Basilica ta' Santa Injazju), an impressive example of Baroque architecture. The bastions of Senglea also provide an excellent vantage point to admire the Grand Harbour and the surrounding islands.

Bormla, or Cospicua, is the largest of the three towns and an important historic port of Malta. The city has a rich maritime tradition and is home to numerous shipyards and dry docks. While walking through the alleys of Bormla, visitors can admire the impressive architecture, including magnificent palaces and churches. St. George's Basilica in Bormla is a remarkable religious building known for its beauty and history.

These three historic towns are not only places of historical significance, but also vibrant communities where Maltese culture and tradition live on. Its narrow streets, picturesque squares and historic buildings tell stories of brave defenders, brave sailors and a rich past. They are places of pride and identity for the people of Malta and an indispensable part of the islands' heritage. The Three Cities invite visitors to immerse themselves in the history of Malta and discover the beauty and significance of these unique places.

The megalithic temples of Ħaġar Qim and Mnajdra

The megalithic temples of Ħaġar Qim and Mnajdra are impressive prehistoric monuments on the Maltese island of Malta. These extraordinary archaeological sites are among the oldest free-standing temples in the world and are a fascinating testament to early human civilization on the Maltese islands.

Located on the southern coast of Malta, the temple complex of Ħaġar Qim consists of a group of stone structures built from huge megaliths. This temple complex was built between 3600 and 3200 BC, making it older than the Egyptian pyramids and Stonehenge in England. Ħaġar Qim consists of several temples, of which the main temple is the most impressive and well-preserved building.

The precise construction and monumental size of the megaliths in Ħaġar Qim are astonishing. The temples are oriented to direct the sun's rays directly into the temple courtyard during the summer solstice, indicating a deep understanding of astronomy and sophisticated construction.

Just a short walk from Ħaġar Qim is the temple complex of Mnajdra. It also consists of several temples, including the main temple of Mnajdra, which also has impressive megalithic structures. The temples of Mnajdra were built around the same time as Ħaġar Qim and have similar astronomical orientations.

These prehistoric temples probably served religious purposes and may have been used as places for ritual ceremonies, worship of deities, or astronomical observations. However, the exact meaning and purpose of these temples remain a mystery and are the subject of scientific research and speculation.

The megalithic temples of Ħaġar Qim and Mnajdra are not only a testimony to the craftsmanship of Neolithic people, but also a testament to their deep-rooted spirituality and understanding of nature. These ancient sites are now an important part of Malta's cultural heritage and were declared a World Heritage Site by UNESCO in 1980.

Visitors will have the opportunity to explore these amazing temples and be captivated by their splendor and mystery. The megalithic temples of Ħaġar Qim and Mnajdra are a fascinating chapter in Malta's history and a window into humanity's past. They are a place of awe and a monument to the early civilizations that inhabited the Maltese islands thousands of years ago.

Gozo: Malta's sister island

Gozo, the second largest of the Maltese islands, is a pearl of the Mediterranean and Malta's natural sister island. Located just a short ferry ride from the main island, it has a unique identity as well as a rich history and culture that attracts visitors from all over the world.

The history of Gozo dates back to ancient times. The island was inhabited by various civilizations, including the Phoenicians, Romans, Byzantines and Arabs, before coming under the rule of the Order of Malta in 1265. This chequered history has left its mark on the island, which can be seen in the ruins, fortresses and historical sites.

One of the most impressive sights in Gozo is the Citadel of Victoria, also known as Rabat. Perched on top of a hill, this ancient fortress offers stunning panoramic views of the island and the surrounding sea. The citadel has served various purposes over the centuries, from defensive purposes to escaping from pirate raids. Today, it is home to museums, historic buildings, and a vibrant community.

Gozo is also known for its prehistoric sites, including the Ggantija Temples, which are among the oldest free-standing temples in the world. These impressive megalithic structures are a testament to the early civilizations that lived in Gozo thousands of years ago. The sites are of great historical and archaeological significance and attract researchers and history buffs alike.

The natural beauty of Gozo is undeniable. The island is characterized by a diverse landscape, ranging from fertile valleys to rolling hills and rocky coasts. One of the most well-known natural attractions is the Azure Window, an impressive natural rock arch on the coast, but it collapsed in 2017 as a result of a storm. Despite this, the coast of

Gozo still offers many spectacular views and rocky coves that invite you to swim and dive.

Maltese culture and tradition are alive and well in Gozo and are maintained by the locals. The island is known for its handmade products, including lace work, ceramics, and local delicacies. Maltese cuisine is particularly appreciated in Gozo, and visitors can enjoy local specialties such as goat cheese, fresh seafood, and traditional pastries.

The relaxed atmosphere and unspoiled nature make Gozo a popular destination for those seeking relaxation and nature lovers. The island offers hiking trails, bike paths, and opportunities for water sports such as diving and snorkeling. The quiet villages and picturesque towns invite you to stroll and explore.

Gozo, Malta's sister island, is a place of natural beauty, rich history and vibrant culture. Its unique identity and charming atmosphere make it a sought-after destination for travelers who want to experience the diversity of the Maltese islands. The locals' love for their island is palpable, and they warmly welcome visitors to discover and enjoy the wonders of Gozo.

Comino: The small island of the Blue Lagoon

Comino, the smallest of Malta's inhabited islands, may be tiny, but it holds a treasure trove of natural beauty and fascinating history. Located between Malta and Gozo, this island is best known for its stunning Blue Lagoon and pristine surroundings.

The history of Comino goes back a long way, and the island has been inhabited by different civilizations over the centuries. It probably owes its name to the cumin plants that once grew here. However, the population of Comino is very small, and the island has only a handful of permanent residents.

The main attraction of Comino is undoubtedly the Blue Lagoon. This idyllic natural harbour is known for its crystal clear turquoise waters and picturesque surroundings. The Blue Lagoon is a popular spot for swimming, snorkeling, and sunbathing. The shallow waters and colorful underwater world make it a paradise for water sports enthusiasts and nature lovers.

However, Comino offers more than just the Blue Lagoon. The island is characterized by unspoiled scenery and offers hiking trails and nature trails that allow visitors to explore the wild beauties of the island. The rocky coasts of Comino are impressive, and there are numerous viewpoints from which to enjoy spectacular views of the Mediterranean Sea.

Another notable sight on Comino is the Santa Maria Tower, a historic watchtower built in the 17th century. The tower was once used to protect the coast from pirate raids and is a testament to the turbulent past of the Maltese islands.

Despite its small size and small population, Comino has a rich flora and fauna. The island is an important breeding ground for birds and is home to a variety of plant and animal species. Bird lovers will find an abundance of species here, including shearwaters, herons, and hawks.

Comino also offers accommodation for those who want to enjoy the tranquil atmosphere and natural beauty of the island for longer. A small hotel and some holiday homes are available to visitors.

The small island of Comino is a place of rest and escape from the hustle and bustle of everyday life. Its peaceful surroundings and impressive nature make it a place to relax and enjoy nature. The Blue Lagoon and pristine landscapes are a magnet for travelers who want to experience the beauty and tranquility of this small island paradise. Comino is undoubtedly a jewel in the Maltese archipelago and a place that enchants visitors with its unique atmosphere and natural beauty.

The Blue Grotto: A Natural Wonder Point

The Blue Grotto, or "Għar Ħasan" in Maltese, is undoubtedly one of Malta's most spectacular natural wonders. This impressive cave, located on the coast of the island of Malta, is a nature lover's paradise and delights visitors from all over the world with its breathtaking beauty.

The Blue Grotto is known for its deep blue waters, illuminated by a clear blue sky and the reflective surface of the sea. The result is a fascinating play of light and colour that transforms the grotto into a magical realm. The colors and shades of the water range from bright turquoise to deep cobalt blue, creating a surreally beautiful environment.

Visitors can explore the Blue Grotto on boat tours departing from various locations in Malta. While driving through the narrow entrances of the cave, a breathtaking underwater world suddenly opens up. The clear waters allow visitors to admire the fascinating underwater landscape, including seabeds, rock formations, and a variety of marine life.

However, the Blue Grotto is not only known for its beauty, but also for its geological formation. It was formed by the erosion of limestone cliffs over millions of years. The result is a complex cave system that amazes visitors. The grotto consists of a series of chambers and tunnels that extend below the surface of the sea.

The Blue Grotto is not only a natural spectacle, but also a place of historical importance. In ancient times, it was visited by Romans and Phoenicians, who used it for religious rituals and offerings. Later, the grotto also served as a hideout for pirates who roamed the Maltese waters.

However, the Blue Grotto is not always accessible. The best conditions to admire their beauty are on clear, sunny days, when the light is most intense and the colors appear most vivid. In the winter months or when the sea is rough, access to the grotto may be restricted.

For nature lovers, photographers and adventurers, the Blue Grotto is an unforgettable experience. Its mesmerizing beauty and geological history make it one of Malta's most remarkable natural attractions. A visit to the Blue Grotto is a journey into a world of colors and wonders that captivates every visitor and leaves a lasting impression.

The fortified city of Mdina: The silent heart of Malta

Mdina, also known as "the silent city", is undoubtedly one of Malta's most fascinating and historic cities. Perched on a hill in the centre of the island, this ancient fortified town proudly carries its rich history and is a living monument to Malta's past.

The history of Mdina goes back a long way, and the city was once the capital of Malta before being superseded by Valletta. Its origins date back to the Phoenician period, and the city has seen many civilizations over the centuries, including the Romans, Byzantines, Arabs, and Normans. This rich historical background can be felt in the narrow streets, imposing walls and historic buildings of Mdina.

One of the most notable features of Mdina is its massive city walls that surround the city, making it look like a fortress from times gone by. These walls were reinforced during the Arab rule and later extended by the Knights of the Order of Malta to protect the city from attacks. Mdina's impressive city gates, including the Main Gate and the Greeks Gate, are impressive testimonies to these historic defenses.

In the narrow streets of Mdina, visitors can immerse themselves in the past. The city is known for its well-preserved palaces and noble residences from the Middle Ages and the Renaissance. Palazzo Falson, also known as Norman House, is an outstanding example of Maltese aristocratic architecture and now houses a museum that gives insights into life in centuries past.

One of the most significant sights of Mdina is St. Paul's Cathedral. This impressive baroque church was built on the foundations of an older church and, according to tradition, is the place where the Apostle Paul died in 60 AD. when he was shipwrecked in Malta. The cathedral houses valuable works of art and religious relics.

However, Mdina is not only a museum of history, but also a lively place. A few locals and shops have set up shop in the town, and there are also some cosy restaurants and cafes where you can enjoy traditional Maltese cuisine.

Visitors to Mdina will be enchanted by the tranquility and timeless charm of the city. The streets are often quiet, and the town offers stunning views of the surrounding countryside. Walking through the cobblestone streets of Mdina is like stepping back in time, an opportunity to experience and appreciate Malta's rich history.

The fortified city of Mdina, the silent heart of Malta, is a place of historical significance and timeless beauty. Its fortress walls and historic buildings tell stories of conquests and wars, while its quiet alleys and squares create an atmosphere of serenity and nostalgia. Mdina is a place where history comes alive and invites visitors to immerse themselves in Malta's fascinating past.

The Maltese folk festivals and celebrations

The Maltese are known for their vibrant culture and enthusiasm for celebrations and festivals. These events play an important role in Malta's social life and are an opportunity for locals to celebrate their traditions and invite visitors from all over the world to take part in the festive activities.

One of the most famous and colourful festivals in Malta is the festival in honour of Saint John, also known as "Festa San Ġwann". This festival is celebrated on June 24 and is one of the most important religious events in the country. The main attractions are the elaborately decorated processions, in which a statue of St. John is carried through the streets. Fireworks, music and traditional dances are also part of these joyful celebrations.

Another outstanding event is the Carnival season, which is celebrated in the days leading up to Lent. During this time, the streets of Malta are filled with colourful parades, elaborate costumes and music. Especially in Valletta and Nadur in Gozo, the carnival festivities are particularly spectacular.

Easter is another highlight in the Maltese festival calendar. The religious processions and services are of great importance, and the locals often carry huge statues through the streets to depict the events of the Passion of Christ.

In addition to the religious festivals, there are also a variety of traditional village festivals where locals celebrate their local patron saints. These festivities include processions, music, dances, and culinary delights prepared specifically for each event.

Another notable celebration is the "Notte Bianca" or the "White Night" in Valletta. This event transforms the streets of the capital into a vibrant arts and culture scene, with concerts, theatrical performances, art exhibitions, and much more that brings the city to life until the early hours of the morning.

The Maltese folk festivals and celebrations are an important expression of Malta's cultural identity. Not only do they offer locals a chance to preserve and celebrate their traditions, but they also give visitors a glimpse of the country's vibrant culture and sense of community. The vibrant colours, music and cheerfulness of these events make them unforgettable experiences for anyone visiting Malta.

The tradition of Carnival in Malta

The Carnival season, or "Carnival" in Maltese, is one of the most exciting and colourful times in the Maltese festival calendar. This traditional festival, celebrated in the days leading up to Lent, is characterised by lively parades, boisterous street parties and elaborate costumes that transform the streets of Malta and Gozo into a colourful spectacle.

The roots of Carnival in Malta go back a long way and have their origins in the religious celebrations of the Middle Ages. The original carnival customs were strongly influenced by the Catholic tradition and served to have fun and consume excess food before the upcoming Lent. It was also during this period that the magnificent carnival costumes and masks were worn to disguise the identity of the celebrants.

One of the unique traditions of the Maltese Carnival is the "Il-Ġostra", a huge wooden mast that is lavishly decorated and erected in the towns and villages. Brave participants try to climb the mast to win prizes. This spectacular event attracts spectators from all over the world.

The Maltese Carnival parades are a highlight of the festivities. Valletta, the capital of Malta, and Nadur in Gozo host impressive parades with elaborate floats, fanciful costumes and masked dancers lining the streets. The parades are often accompanied by music, and the sounds of brass bands and drummers fill the air.

The costumes worn during the Maltese Carnival are often ornately designed, ranging from historical figures to modern pop culture icons. Contestants invest a lot of time and creativity into their costumes, and it's not uncommon to see groups of friends or families present themselves in coordinated outfits.

During the carnival season, there are also numerous street festivals and concerts where people come together to party and dance. The atmosphere is exuberant and cheerful, and there is a lot of dancing, laughing and partying.

The tradition of Carnival in Malta is a time of joy and expression. It unites the Maltese people in a common celebration of joie de vivre and creative self-expression. Visitors who travel to Malta during this time will have the opportunity to take part in one of the country's most exciting and colourful festivals and experience the island's vibrant culture in all its glory. The Maltese Carnival is a tradition that warms people's hearts and provides an unforgettable experience for everyone who participates.

The Maltese Music Scene: From Għana to Modern Pop Music

The Maltese music scene is a fascinating kaleidoscope of cultural diversity and artistic expression. From traditional folk music to contemporary pop sounds, Malta has a rich musical history that combines influences from different eras and regions.

One of the most notable genres of Maltese music is "Għana". Often referred to as "Maltese folk music", this form of song is deeply rooted in Maltese culture. Għana are lyrical songs that are often accompanied by traditional Maltese lute instruments. These songs tell stories from people's lives, their sorrows, joys and experiences. They are an expression of Maltese identity and an important part of the country's folklore.

Throughout history, Malta has also absorbed a variety of musical influences from the Mediterranean and Europe. Italian music, especially opera, had a strong influence on the Maltese musical tradition. Malta also has a rich history of choral music, dating back to the Middle Ages. Choirs are important cultural institutions on the island and regularly perform concerts.

In modern times, the Maltese music scene has evolved to encompass a wide range of genres. Pop music has grown in prominence over the past few decades, and Malta has produced some talented pop artists who have found success both nationally and internationally. The annual

"Malta Song Festival", which attracts artists from all over the world, is a testament to Malta's modern music scene.

A notable highlight in modern Maltese music history was winning the Eurovision Song Contest in 2002. Maltese singer Ira Losco took second place, helping to put Malta on the international music scene. This success was a milestone for Maltese pop music and led to increased recognition of the country's music scene.

The Maltese music scene is now more diverse than ever, and musicians from Malta are using their artistic diversity to wow the world. The cultural mix reflected in Maltese music is an important part of the country's identity and reflects the openness and tolerance of Maltese society.

From the traditional sounds of Għana to modern pop music, the Maltese music scene has made a fascinating journey. It is a reflection of Malta's history and culture and a living expression of the island's artistic creativity. The Maltese music scene will undoubtedly continue to grow and develop, touching the hearts of music lovers in Malta and beyond.

The Maltese Art Scene: From Caravaggio to the Present

The Maltese art scene is a fascinating journey through the centuries, rich in cultural diversity and creative expression. From the early influences of great masters such as Caravaggio to the vibrant contemporary art scene, Malta has a rich history of art that captures the essence of Maltese identity.

One of the most well-known names closely associated with Maltese art history is Michelangelo Merisi da Caravaggio. The Italian baroque painter lived in Malta for a time and left a significant artistic influence here. His works, including the impressive painting "The Beheading of John the Baptist", can still be admired today at St. John's Co-Cathedral Museum in Valletta. Caravaggio brought an innovative realistic depiction of light and shadow to art, which had a lasting impact on the Maltese art scene.

During the 17th and 18th centuries, Malta experienced a heyday of Baroque art. The country's magnificent churches and palaces were adorned with stunning paintings, sculptures, and frescoes. The work of local artists such as Mattia Preti and Francesco Zahra helped to cement Malta's religious and cultural identity.

In the 19th century, Maltese art continued to develop, and artists such as Giuseppe Hyzler and Gianni Vella gained notoriety. The works of these artists reflected the Romantic era, depicting the picturesque beauty of the islands as well as the lives of the people.

The Maltese art scene of the 20th century produced a variety of styles and artists. Artists such as Antoine Camilleri and Esprit Barthet continued their creative work and left their mark on the art scene during this era. The Maltese Academy of Fine Arts was founded in 1923 and played a crucial role in promoting art education and development on the islands.

The contemporary art scene in Malta is now more vibrant than ever. A new generation of artists, including Mark Mallia and Norbert Attard, has taken the stage, showcasing a wide range of styles and techniques. Modern galleries and art centres provide platforms for artists to showcase their work to the public, and Malta has become a major centre for contemporary art in the Mediterranean.

The Maltese art scene has undergone an impressive evolution over the centuries. From the masters of the Renaissance and Baroque to the vibrant contemporary art scene, it showcases the creative energy and diversity of the artists who have worked on these islands. Art remains an important expression of Maltese identity and a source of inspiration for artists and art lovers from all over the world.

Religion in Malta: From Roman times to the present day

Malta's religious history is marked by a variety of faiths and cultures that have influenced the islands over the centuries. From Roman times to the present day, Malta's religious landscape reflects changing political and cultural influences.

In ancient times, Malta was an important crossroads in the Roman Empire, and Roman religion, based on the worship of gods and goddesses, was widespread. Temples and sanctuaries were built on the island to pay homage to the Roman gods, and some of these archaeological sites are still visible today, including the temples of Ħaġar Qim and Mnajdra.

With the rise of Christianity in the Roman Empire, Malta became an important center of Christianity. According to tradition, the apostle Paul was shipped to Malta in 60 AD when his ship was shipwrecked off the coast. This event led to the spread of Christianity on the island. The Maltese population embraced Christianity, and a strong Christian tradition developed that continues to this day.

During Arab rule in the Middle Ages, Islam was introduced to Malta, and there are still traces of this period in the Maltese language and culture. Malta's multilingual identity is visible in its religious diversity, and the Christian faith remained the dominant religion.

The conquest of Malta by the Knights of the Order of Malta in the 16th century led to the strengthening of the Catholic faith on the island. The Maltese were known for their defense of Christianity against the threat of the Ottoman Empire, and they played a crucial role in spreading and preserving the Catholic faith.

During British rule in the 19th and 20th centuries, Malta became an important stronghold of the Catholic faith in the region. The Catholic Church was, and still is, a dominant religious institution that influences daily life and celebrations on the islands.

Today, Malta is a predominantly Catholic country, and the Catholic Church plays a significant role in social and cultural life. However, in addition to Catholicism, there are other faiths on the island, including Protestant churches, Orthodox communities, and a growing Muslim population.

Religion in Malta is a reflection of the islands' turbulent history and cultural diversity. From the Roman gods to Christianity and the various faiths of the present, the religious landscape reflects Malta's deep-rooted identity and openness to different faiths.

Maltese folklore and customs

Maltese folklore and customs are a fascinating aspect of Maltese culture that is deeply rooted in the country's history and identity. These lore and rituals reflect the rich cultural diversity and vibrant community on the Maltese islands.

One of the most famous Maltese folklores is the "Festa", a traditional village festival celebrated in honour of a patron saint. Every town and village in Malta has its own patron saint, and the festas are lively events that often coincide with religious processions, music, fireworks, and traditional dances. These festas attract not only the locals, but also visitors from all over the world, who take the opportunity to immerse themselves in the colorful festivities.

An important part of Maltese folklore is the "giganti" or giant figures, which play a central role in festas. These huge, human-borne figures often represent biblical or historical characters and are carried through the streets during processions. The Giganti are intricately designed and worn by dedicated parishioners who take pride in preserving their traditions.

The "fenkata" is another popular custom in Maltese folklore. This traditional rabbit race often takes place during the Easter season and is very popular with locals and tourists alike. The reindeer are not rabbits, but specially made wooden figures pulled by young men. The race is an exciting event where the village community comes together to cheer on their favourites.

The "Għonnella" is a traditional Maltese wedding dress often worn by newlyweds in rural areas. This historic garment is intricately embroidered, reflecting the rich craftsmanship and tradition. Wedding celebrations in Malta are often accompanied by traditional dances, music, and festive customs that celebrate the bond of family and community.

Maltese folklore and customs are an important part of Malta's cultural heritage. They connect people with their history, their roots and their fellow human beings. These living traditions are passed down from generation to generation and are a testament to the rich culture and close-knit community that exists in the Maltese Islands. Maltese folklore is a treasure that reflects Malta's identity in all its diversity and colourfulness.

Maltese craftsmanship and the art of filigree

The art of filigree is an outstanding example of craftsmanship and cultural significance in Malta. This artful technique of wire bending and interweaving has a long history in the Maltese Islands and has become an important cultural heritage.

The origins of filigree craftsmanship in Malta can be traced back to the Phoenician period, indicating a tradition that goes back thousands of years. Filigree craftsmanship has been passed down and refined from generation to generation over the centuries. It is a technique in which thin wires of gold or silver are carefully bent and braided to create intricate and ornate pieces of jewelry.

The intricate filigree works are often decorated with patterns and motifs that reflect Maltese culture and history. Popular motifs include Maltese crosses, doves and other symbols of religious significance. These pieces of jewellery are not only ornate, but also have a deep spiritual meaning for the people of Malta.

The filigree craftsmanship requires a high degree of skill and patience. The artists and craftsmen who master this art often spend many hours bending and shaping tiny pieces of wire to create ornate pieces of jewelry. It is a traditional technique that has become rare in the modern world, but continues to be nurtured and appreciated in Malta.

The intricate pieces of jewellery are not only popular in Malta, but are also appreciated by visitors who want to experience the island's unique craftsmanship. Not only are these gems beautiful to look at, but they are also a significant cultural heritage that celebrates Malta's history and artistry.

In addition, Maltese craftsmanship is not limited to the art of filigree. There is a wide range of artisanal traditions on the islands, from ceramics and textiles to woodwork and glassblowing. These crafts reflect the diversity and talent of Maltese artisans and are an important part of Maltese culture and economy.

Overall, the Maltese craft and art of filigree is an expression of creativity, skill and cultural pride. The filigree pieces of jewellery are not only ornate accessories, but also a link to Malta's rich history and culture. They are a testament to the artistry and passion of the people of the Maltese islands.

The Maltese Language: Insight into Maltese

The Maltese language, also known as "Maltese" or "Il-Lingwa Maltija," is a fascinating part of Maltese culture and identity. As the only Semitic language officially recognized in the European Union, Maltese has undergone a unique history and development.

The roots of Maltese go far back in history. It evolved from Arabic, which was brought to the islands during the Arab rule of Malta from the 9th to the 13th century. These Arabic influences are still evident in the Maltese language, especially in words and phrases borrowed from Arabic.

However, Maltese has undergone an astonishing evolution over the centuries and has been heavily influenced by other languages, including Italian, English and French. This is due to the changing political rulers of Malta, which led to a cultural mix and influenced the language.

The Maltese language uses the Latin alphabet and has a unique grammar and syntax. It is a mixture of Semitic and Romance language structure, making it a challenging but fascinating language. Maltese also has many loanwords from Italian, which makes it easier to understand for speakers of this language.

Although Maltese is the official language of Malta, English is also widely spoken and is present in many areas of daily life. Due to its history as a British colony and its current membership in the Commonwealth of Nations, English is an important second language for the Maltese.

The Maltese language is closely linked to Malta's cultural identity. It is taught in schools and used in the media, government, and everyday life. Maltese is also the language of literature and art on the islands, and there is a rich tradition of Maltese poetry and prose.

Over the past few decades, the Maltese language has undergone a steady development and is still alive and vital. Efforts are being made to promote and protect the language to ensure that it continues to play an important role in Malta in the future.

The Maltese language is a remarkable example of cultural diversity and linguistic diversity. It is an integral part of the Maltese identity and a reflection of the changing cultural influences that have shaped the history of the islands. Maltese is not just a language, but a window into Malta's rich history and culture, proudly worn by the locals.

The School System and Education in Malta

The education system in Malta is an important part of Maltese society and plays a crucial role in preparing the young generation for a successful future. Malta has made significant strides in the field of education over the years and has developed a diverse range of educational offerings.

The school system in Malta is divided into different levels. Primary education is compulsory and lasts for six years, starting at the age of five. Primary schools offer a wide range of curriculum covering core subjects such as Mathematics, Maltese, English, Science and Social Sciences. The curriculum also emphasizes the promotion of cultural awareness, language skills, and social skills.

After primary education, students have the opportunity to transfer to secondary schools. Secondary education in Malta lasts for five years and leads to the O-level and A-level exams offered by the University of Cambridge. These exams are of international recognition and allow graduates to enter colleges and universities worldwide.

Malta also has a wide range of vocational schools and educational institutions geared towards specialized vocational training and skills. These schools offer programs in areas such as engineering, commerce, healthcare, and tourism, preparing students for professional careers.

Higher education in Malta is offered by various institutions, including the University of Malta, which is the largest and oldest university in the country. The University of Malta offers a wide range of bachelor's and master's degree programs in various disciplines and also attracts international students.

Education in Malta is free and accessible to all, regardless of the financial situation of the families. The Maltese government invests significant resources in the education system to ensure that the quality of education is high and that students are prepared for their future in the best possible way.

Another important aspect of the Maltese education system is multilingualism. Maltese is the official language of the country, but English is widely spoken and taught. This is due to Malta's colonial past, when English played an important role. This multilingualism opens up many opportunities for graduates in an international context.

In addition to formal education, Malta has a rich cultural and artistic scene that fosters students' creativity and artistic abilities. There are numerous art schools, music schools and cultural events that promote the talents of the young generation.

The education system in Malta has evolved over the years, providing students with a solid foundation for their personal and professional development. It is an important cornerstone of Maltese society and a key to creating a promising future for generations to come. Malta is committed to maximising educational opportunities for all and ensuring that education is a pathway to success and personal fulfilment.

Medical care in Malta

Medical care in Malta is of high quality and accessible to locals as well as tourists. The country's healthcare system has evolved over the years, offering a wide range of services to meet the needs of the population.

The Maltese healthcare system is based on a public and private healthcare sector. The Public Health Service is run by the government and provides free medical care to all Maltese citizens and residents. This service includes hospitals, health centers, and clinics that offer a variety of medical services.

Mater Dei Hospital in Msida is the largest hospital in Malta and an important part of the public healthcare system. It has state-of-the-art medical facilities and provides services in various medical specialties, including surgery, obstetrics, pediatrics, and emergency medicine. The hospital is well equipped and has highly qualified medical staff.

Medical care in Malta also includes a wide range of specialized medical services. There are specialists in fields such as cardiology, neurology, oncology, gastroenterology, and more. These specialists provide diagnosis and treatment for complex medical conditions.

In addition to the public healthcare system, there is also a private healthcare sector in Malta that offers paid medical services. Private hospitals and clinics can be found in different parts of the islands, providing an additional option for those who prefer private medical care.

Malta has a well-trained medical workforce, including doctors, nurses, and caregivers. Medical education in Malta meets international standards, and many Maltese doctors have perfected their training abroad. This ensures the quality of medical care in the country.

Medical care in Malta also extends to preventive health measures. There are programs for health promotion and early detection of diseases that are supported by the government. Vaccinations and screenings are widely available and play an important role in maintaining the health of the population.

Emergency clinics and medical services are available for tourists who need medical care in Malta. Most doctors and medical professionals speak English, which makes communication easier.

In conclusion, medical care in Malta is of high quality and easily accessible. The combination of the public and private healthcare sectors, highly qualified professionals and modern medical facilities ensures comprehensive care for the people of Malta. The health of the people of the Maltese islands is seen as an important aspect of well-being and quality of life, and the country is committed to maintaining this high level of health care.

Maltese legal system and justice

The Maltese legal system and the judiciary are of great importance for order and stability in Malta. They form the legal backbone of Maltese society and are an integral part of the country's democracy.

The Maltese legal system is based on a mixed system of civil law and common law. This is the result of the historical developments that Malta has undergone over the centuries. The Maltese legal system is based on a constitution that protects the rights and freedoms of citizens and ensures the separation of powers between the various organs of government.

The Maltese judiciary is independent and led by professionals in the field of law. The court system includes various judicial instances, including the civil court, the criminal court, and the constitutional court. The highest court is the Supreme Court of Malta, which acts as the highest appellate court in legal matters.

The Maltese legal framework covers a wide range of areas of law, including civil law, criminal law, commercial law, employment law, environmental law, and many others. Maltese jurisprudence is primarily codified in writing and is based on laws enacted by Parliament. In addition, precedents and court rulings play an important role in the interpretation and application of the law.

The administration of justice in Malta is based on fairness and justice. Citizens have the right to a fair trial and a defence in court. Lawyers play a crucial role in assisting parties in legal matters.

The Maltese judiciary also has mechanisms for resolving disputes outside the courts, such as arbitration and alternative dispute resolution methods. These approaches promote faster and more cost-effective resolution of conflicts.

Malta's legal system is also closely linked to the European legal framework, as Malta is a member of the European Union. This means that Maltese law is in line with EU law and is supervised by the EU institutions.

In terms of criminal law and law enforcement, there is a police and law enforcement agency in Malta that is responsible for maintaining public order and security. Malta's penal laws are designed with the safety of citizens in mind and aim to prevent and prosecute crimes.

In conclusion, the Maltese legal system and judiciary play an important role in upholding the rule of law and justice in Malta. They provide citizens with protection from rights violations and contribute to the stability and democracy of the country. The Maltese Government strives to ensure the independence and efficiency of the judiciary and to ensure that the legal system meets the needs of society.

Malta's Economy: From Tourism to the Financial Industry

Malta's economy has undergone remarkable transformation in recent decades, becoming a diverse and growing force in the region. This economic recovery is the result of targeted policies and a broad diversification of the economy.

Tourism plays a prominent role in the Maltese economy. The Maltese islands attract millions of tourists every year who enjoy the rich history, stunning coastal scenery and warm Mediterranean atmosphere. The tourism industry provides jobs for thousands of Maltese and contributes significantly to the gross domestic product.

The financial industry has also become an important sector of the economy. Malta has become an attractive location for international financial services companies, benefiting from the country's stable political and economic environment. This has helped create jobs and encourage investment in the Maltese economy.

Information and communication technology (ICT) is another emerging sector in Malta. The country has made considerable efforts to attract ICT companies and expand digital infrastructure. This has contributed to the creation of highly skilled jobs and the promotion of innovation in the economy.

The manufacturing industry in Malta includes sectors such as pharmaceuticals, electronics, and shipbuilding. These industries have seen solid growth in recent years and contribute to the country's export diversity.

Agriculture in Malta has become a smaller sector due to limited agricultural land and water resources. Nevertheless, agricultural production continues on the islands, and various products such as olives, wine and vegetables are grown.

Malta has also made efforts to promote renewable energy and reduce dependence on fossil fuels. This is part of the country's efforts to use sustainable and environmentally friendly energy sources.

The unemployment rate in Malta is relatively low compared to other European countries, and employment opportunities are good. The Maltese government has implemented workforce skills and upskilling programmes to ensure that the population is equipped to meet the demands of the labour market.

Malta's economic stability has made the country an attractive destination for foreign investors. There is a well-established infrastructure for foreign direct investment and incentives that attract investors.

Overall, it can be said that Malta's economy is characterized by broad diversification and a consistent pursuit of economic growth. The Maltese government is committed to maximizing economic opportunities and ensuring that the economy continues to thrive in the years to come.

Maltese Architecture: A Journey Through the Centuries

Malta's architecture is a fascinating kaleidoscope of history, spanning centuries and showing influences from different eras and cultures. This architectural diversity is a reflection of Malta's chequered history and its strategic location in the Mediterranean.

The oldest traces of human architecture on the Maltese islands date back to the time of the megalithic temples, built between 3600 and 2500 BC. These prehistoric temples, including Ħaġar Qim and Mnajdra, are among the oldest free-standing structures in the world and bear witness to a highly developed culture that existed on the islands.

In ancient times, Malta was occupied by Phoenicians, Romans and Byzantines, and these conquerors left their architectural traces. The Roman villas and baths bear witness to the Roman presence on the islands.

One of the most significant architectural periods in Malta's history was the time of the Knights of the Order of St. John, also known as the Knights of Malta. They ruled from 1530 to 1798 and had a significant influence on the architecture of Malta. The capital city of Valletta, founded by the Knights, is an outstanding example of Renaissance and Baroque architecture. The fortified city of Mdina, also known as "the silent city", is another gem of medieval architecture.

In the 19th century, Malta underwent another architectural transformation under British rule. The British left behind neoclassical-style buildings, including government buildings, churches, and residences. The influence of the British Empire can be seen in many aspects of Maltese architecture.

Malta's independence in 1964 led to a modern architectural boom. In recent decades, numerous modern buildings and infrastructure facilities have been erected that have changed the cityscape. Nevertheless, care is taken to preserve the historical heritage and to promote the integration of old and new.

Maltese architecture also reflects the country's religious diversity. In addition to Catholic churches, there are also Anglican churches, mosques and synagogues that bear witness to Malta's multicultural society.

Overall, Maltese architecture is a rich heritage that reflects the country's history and culture. Preserving this heritage and fostering contemporary architectural innovation go hand in hand to shape and enrich Malta's architectural landscape. This diversity and historical depth make Malta's architecture a fascinating subject for explorers and lovers of architecture.

The Maltese Transport System: From Buses to Ferries

Malta's transport system is an integral part of daily life on the islands and plays a crucial role in the mobility of locals and tourists. Malta, consisting of the main islands of Malta, Gozo and Comino, has a well-developed and efficient transport network that allows people to move around the islands.

The main mode of transport in Malta is road transport. The island of Malta has a dense network of roads and highways that connect the different cities and towns. The road network is well maintained and allows for a smooth flow of traffic. However, there are also some challenges, including limited space and occasional traffic congestion.

Public transport in Malta is mainly operated by buses. The Maltese bus network is extensive, connecting almost all parts of the islands. The buses are usually modern and air-conditioned, making them a convenient transportation option for locals and tourists. Public transport plays an important role in reducing traffic and environmental impact.

In addition to bus transport, there are also taxis, which are widely available on the islands. These offer a flexible way to get around within towns and villages. Taxis can be ordered at official taxi ranks as well as by phone or via apps.

Another important component of Malta's transport system is the ferry connection between the islands of Malta and Gozo.

The ferries are a vital link for Gozo residents, allowing them to commute between islands quickly and easily. The ferries also offer a scenic way for tourists to enjoy the beauty of the Mediterranean.

Cycling is also popular in Malta and is practiced by locals and tourists alike. There are bike paths and rental stations on the island that make cycling safe and accessible.

In addition, Malta has an international airport that makes it easy for tourists from all over the world to get there. Malta International Airport offers a wide range of flight connections and is a major entry and exit point for the islands.

To sum up, Malta's transport system is diverse and well-developed. It allows people to move around the islands comfortably and plays a crucial role in the country's economic development and tourism. The Maltese authorities are actively working to improve transport infrastructure and promote sustainable means of transport to facilitate mobility in the region.

Outdoor activities: scuba diving, hiking, and more

The Maltese Islands offer an abundance of outdoor activities for nature lovers and adventurers. With their Mediterranean climate and stunning coastal scenery, Malta, Gozo and Comino are a paradise for those who want to explore the beauty of nature.

Scuba diving is one of the most popular outdoor activities in the Maltese Islands. The waters around Malta are some of the best diving in the Mediterranean. The clear and warm waters are home to a rich marine fauna and flora. Divers can explore shipwrecks from centuries past, including the famous wreck of HMS Maori off the coast of Valletta. There are numerous diving schools and centers that offer diving trips and courses for beginners and experienced divers.

Hiking is another popular activity in the Maltese Islands. The countryside offers a variety of hiking trails and routes that pass through picturesque villages, along the coast and through unspoiled nature. The island of Gozo is particularly known for its hiking opportunities, including the famous coastal path, which offers stunning views of the sea. The mild climate makes it possible to hike all year round, with spring and autumn being particularly pleasant seasons.

In addition to diving and hiking, water sports such as windsurfing, kitesurfing and sailing are popular in the Maltese islands. The clear waters and constant winds create ideal conditions for these activities.

Malta also offers opportunities for bird watching, especially during the migratory bird season when different species of birds pass through the islands. The salt flats of Malta are an important habitat for migratory birds and a popular spot for ornithologists.

For those who love nature but prefer to stay grounded, the Maltese islands offer rich flora and fauna. There are numerous nature reserves and gardens, including Buskett Gardens and Dingli Cliffs Natural Heritage Park, which offer a glimpse of native flora and fauna.

Overall, outdoor activities in Malta are diverse and varied. They allow visitors to explore the natural beauty of the islands while experiencing adventure and relaxation. Whether underwater, on hiking trails or on a sailboat, the Maltese islands offer unforgettable experiences for outdoor enthusiasts of all kinds.

The Maltese Carnival: From Costumes to Parades

The Carnival in Malta is a joyful and colourful celebration that is celebrated every year and showcases Maltese culture and traditions in all their glory. This traditional festival has a long history and is a time of joy and exuberance for locals and visitors alike.

The Maltese Carnival usually starts in February and lasts for several days. During this time, the streets of the towns and villages are transformed into a lively festival landscape. One of the most famous cities for the carnival festivities is Valletta, the capital of Malta, but other places such as Mdina and Nadur in Gozo are also known for their colourful parades and celebrations.

One of the standout features of the Maltese Carnival is the elaborate costumes worn by the participants. Preparations for these costumes often begin months in advance, and people work hard to express their creativity and craftsmanship. The costumes are often inspired by historical or folkloric themes and are decorated with intricate details and accessories.

Numerous events and activities take place during the carnival, including parades, musical performances, street theatre and dance performances. The parades are undoubtedly one of the highlights of the festival. Colorful floats and groups of dancers parade through the streets, accompanied by music and applause from the spectators.

The parades often tell stories or depict historical events and are a visual spectacle.

A distinctive feature of the Maltese Carnival is the use of grotesque masks known as "Għawma tal-Maskri". Often inspired by satirical characters, these masks are used to humorously comment on social and political issues.

During Carnival, partying and dancing together in the streets is widespread. People come together to share the joy of the festival and there is an exuberant atmosphere that reflects the Maltese hospitality and sense of community.

The Maltese Carnival is an important cultural heritage that shapes the country's identity. It allows people to preserve and celebrate their traditions and attracts numerous visitors from all over the world every year. It is a time of joyful togetherness, when the Maltese proudly present their history and culture while celebrating the joy of life.

Nightlife in Malta: bars, clubs and events

The nightlife in Malta is lively, diverse and has something for everyone. The Maltese islands, especially Malta and Gozo, are known for their vibrant club scene, cosy bars and exciting events. Although the islands are comparatively small, there is no shortage of entertainment options that keep visitors hooked until the early hours of the morning.

In Valletta, the capital of Malta, you will find an abundance of bars and clubs that offer a wide range of music genres and atmospheres. From chic cocktail bars with stunning views to lively nightclubs where you can dance to the latest hits, there's something for everyone. The Maltese club scene is known for its passionate music scene, and international DJs often perform in the hottest clubs.

Sliema and St. Julian's are other hotspots for nightlife in Malta. Here you will find a concentration of bars and clubs that are particularly popular with younger visitors. The Paceville neighborhood in St. Julian's is known for its exciting nightlife and numerous clubs where the party continues until the wee hours of the morning.

For those who like it quieter, Maltese bars also offer cozy corners and pub atmosphere where you can enjoy local beers and wines. You can also try traditional Maltese snacks in many bars, including "pastizzi" (puff pastries) and "hobz biz-zejt" (bread with tomatoes and olive oil).

Nightlife in Malta includes not only clubs and bars, but also a variety of events and festivals that take place throughout the year. These include concerts, open-air film screenings, street festivals and cultural events. The Valletta

International Baroque Festival and the Malta Jazz Festival are just two examples of the diverse events that enliven the islands.

Something unique about nightlife in Malta is the "Festa" - a religious celebration that is often associated with impressive fireworks and music. These festivals take place in various towns and villages and offer a fascinating way to experience Maltese culture and tradition.

To sum up, the nightlife in Malta is a fascinating mix of music, dance, socializing and culture. Whether you want to spend the night in a trendy club or relax in a cozy bar, Malta has something to offer for night owls of all kinds. The lively atmosphere and the hospitality of the locals make the experience of the Maltese nightlife special.

Maltese souvenirs and shopping

Shopping in Malta is not only a way to take home unique souvenirs, but also an opportunity to immerse yourself in Maltese culture and craftsmanship. The Maltese islands offer a variety of shopping opportunities, from traditional markets to modern shopping malls where visitors can discover a wide range of products.

A popular souvenir of Malta is the famous "Filigree" jewellery. The art of filigree has been deeply rooted in the Maltese islands for centuries. They are ornate pieces of jewelry that are made from fine silver or gold wires to create intricate patterns and designs. Filigree jewelry is handmade and is often made in small workshops. Not only are they beautiful, but they are also a piece of Maltese craftsmanship that you can find in many jewellery shops and local markets.

Another traditional craft in Malta is the production of lace. The "Maltese Lace" is known for its delicate patterns and fine workmanship. Often sold in the form of tablecloths, runners, bags, and garments, these laces are an elegant souvenir that represents Malta's artisanal tradition.

If you're looking for culinary souvenirs, consider Maltese honey, olive oil, and traditional sweets like "qubbajt" (nougat) and "kwareżimal." Maltese cuisine is rich in flavours, and these products are ideal souvenirs to take the flavours of Malta home with you.

Markets are also great places to find local products and souvenirs. The Marsaxlokk fish market is famous for its fresh fish offerings and the colorful fishing boats that line the harbor. In Malta's many markets, you can also find handmade textiles, ceramics, glassware and much more.

For those who prefer modern shopping experiences, Malta also offers a variety of shopping malls and boutiques. The Valletta Waterfront and BayStreet Shopping Complex in St. Julian's are popular destinations for fashion, accessories and entertainment.

It's worth noting that Malta is an EU member state, so visitors from outside the European Union can get a refund of Value Added Tax (VAT) on purchases if they meet the required conditions.

Overall, Malta offers a rich variety of souvenirs and shopping opportunities that reflect the culture, crafts and culinary delights of the islands. Whether you're looking for traditional treasures or modern finds, shopping in Malta is an exciting way to discover the treasures of these beautiful islands and take them home with you.

Naturalization in Malta: Life on the Island

Malta, as one of the sun-drenched islands of the Mediterranean, not only attracts tourists from all over the world, but also offers the opportunity for naturalization and living on the island. This process is well-structured and transparent, and Malta has become an attractive destination for expatriates and people looking for permanent residency in a picturesque and vibrant environment in recent years.

To obtain Maltese citizenship, applicants must meet certain criteria and requirements. These criteria may vary, depending on the nationality and circumstances of the applicant, but in general, the following points should be considered:

1. **Residency** in Malta: As a general rule, applicants must have spent a certain amount of time in Malta before they can apply for naturalization. This period can vary, but it is usually at least 12 months.
2. **Integration**: Applicants must demonstrate that they have successfully integrated into Maltese society. This can be done by demonstrating language proficiency, social engagement, and other factors.

3. **Financial stability**: Applicants are expected to have sufficient financial resources to support themselves in Malta without relying on public assistance.
4. **Health** check: In some cases, a health check may be required to ensure that the applicant does not have any communicable diseases.
5. **Criminal record**: Individuals with criminal records or current criminal proceedings may have difficulty obtaining naturalization.

It is important to note that Malta is a member of the European Union, which means that Maltese citizens enjoy the full rights and privileges of an EU member, including freedom of movement within the Schengen area.

Living in Malta offers many advantages, including a mild climate, rich history and culture, a high quality of life, excellent healthcare and well-developed infrastructure. The island also offers a wide range of recreational opportunities, including water sports, hiking, diving, and a thriving arts and culture scene.

Malta is also a tax haven for expatriates, as there is no inheritance tax, capital gains tax, or wealth tax. This makes it an attractive destination for individuals looking to protect and optimize their assets.

In recent years, Malta has also increased its investment in educational institutions, offering a wide range of international schools and universities that offer a world-class education in English.

To sum up, naturalization in Malta is a well-thought-out process that offers the opportunity to live in a beautiful

Mediterranean country with many advantages. Choosing to live in Malta can be an exciting journey that fully embraces the cultural diversity and quality of life of the islands.

Maltese hospitality and the culture of hospitality

Malta, an island nation in the heart of the Mediterranean, is known not only for its stunning scenery and rich history, but also for the exceptional hospitality of its people. The Maltese culture of hospitality is deeply rooted and reflects the values of kindness, generosity and respect.

The Maltese pride themselves on their warm and welcoming nature. As soon as they arrive on the islands, visitors are often greeted by a sense of belonging. Locals are known for welcoming strangers with open arms and taking an interest in their well-being.

An important part of Maltese hospitality is the sharing of meals and shared moments. Maltese cuisine, influenced by Mediterranean influences, plays a central role in the culture. Guests are often invited to delicious home-cooked dishes serving traditional dishes such as 'rabbit stew' or 'pastizzi'. It is customary for hosts to make sure that guests are fed and satisfied.

Maltese hospitality is also evident in the helpfulness and support shown to people in times of need and need. Whether it's lost directions or helping to overcome personal challenges, Maltese are known for helping each other and fostering a strong sense of community.

Another aspect of Maltese hospitality is the willingness to share one's culture and traditions with others. Visitors often have the opportunity to take part in the numerous festivals, celebrations, and events that take place throughout the year. These events offer glimpses of Malta's vibrant and colourful culture, from religious festivals to carnival parades.

The Maltese language, called Maltese, is another expression of the islands' cultural identity and hospitality. Although English is widely spoken and serves as the official language, Maltese is appreciated by locals and is a means of connecting with Malta's history and tradition.

Overall, Maltese hospitality is an integral part of the culture and life on the islands. It helps make Malta a warm and welcoming place for visitors from all over the world. The people of Malta like to open their hearts and their doors and share the beauty and rich experiences of their unique islands.

Sustainability and environmental protection in Malta

The issue of sustainability and environmental protection is of great importance around the world today, and Malta is no exception. As an island nation in the Mediterranean Sea that has inherently limited resources and depends on a thriving tourism industry, Malta has made significant efforts to minimize its environmental impact and promote sustainable practices.

The Maltese government has taken various measures to promote environmental protection on the island. This includes the introduction of laws and regulations on coastal conservation, waste management and nature conservation. The monitoring and protection of nature reserves such as the Ħal-Far Nature Reserve and the islands of Comino and Gozo are of great importance in order to preserve Malta's unique flora and fauna.

The promotion of renewable energy is another focus of Malta's sustainability efforts. The introduction of solar panels on building roofs and the use of wind energy help reduce dependence on fossil fuels and reduce CO_2 emissions.

Waste management is also an important aspect of Malta's sustainability strategy. Waste sorting and recycling programs have been introduced to reduce the burden on landfills and promote the recycling of resources. Visitors and locals are encouraged to actively participate in these efforts by properly disposing of and recycling their garbage.

The Maltese government also works closely with various environmental organizations to protect biodiversity and ecosystems on the islands. This includes the protection of endangered species such as the Malta falcon and the Caretta caretta turtle that nest in Malta.

Another important step towards sustainability is the promotion of environmentally friendly means of transport. This includes the expansion of public transport, the creation of cycle lanes and the introduction of electric vehicles to reduce the environmental impact of transport in Malta.

In addition to the government's efforts, many local businesses and communities are also contributing to sustainable development. Examples include eco-friendly hotels, restaurants that use local products, and initiatives to reduce plastic packaging.

Overall, Malta has made significant progress in the area of sustainability and environmental protection, and efforts to preserve its unique natural environment continue. This is crucial to preserve the islands' beauty and resources for future generations while meeting the needs of the current population.

Future outlook: Where is Malta headed?

Malta has undergone an astonishing transformation in recent decades, becoming a modern and diverse island nation. The question of Malta's future is of interest as the island continues to face challenges, but also offers opportunities for growth and progress.

One of the key issues that will shape Malta's future is sustainability. Efforts to preserve the environment and reduce environmental impacts are expected to continue and intensify. This is necessary to preserve Malta's unique nature and valuable coastal regions, while maintaining the quality of life of residents and attractiveness to tourists.

The tourism industry, which plays a significant role in the Maltese economy, is expected to continue to develop. Malta has established itself as a popular tourist destination, and the increasing number of visitors will lead to new opportunities and challenges. Promoting sustainable tourism that respects Malta's culture and natural beauty will be crucial.

Malta's economy has diversified, and the financial industry has become a major player. The government will continue to work to create a favorable business environment and attract foreign investment. The increasing importance of digital technologies and innovation could make Malta a hub for technology and start-ups in the region.

The challenges in the education system and health care will be addressed to ensure that the needs of the population are met. The promotion of research and development will help to strengthen the knowledge and skills of Maltese citizens.

The issue of migration and the treatment of migrants remains a controversial issue influencing Maltese politics and society. The government will continue to strive to pursue a balanced and equitable policy on migration.

Maltese culture and identity are an integral part of Malta's future prospects. The preservation of the Maltese language, traditions and customs will continue to play an important role, while at the same time Malta remains an open and multicultural society.

Overall, Malta's future prospects are characterised by a dynamic mix of opportunities and challenges. The island nation will continue to evolve, with the preservation of its unique identity and environment being central. Malta will walk its way into the future with confidence and determination, with the needs and aspirations of its citizens and visitors at its core.

Epilogue

With this book, we have taken a fascinating journey through the history, culture, nature and society of Malta. From the prehistoric temples to the modern economy, from the historic cities to the stunning coastal landscapes, we have explored the diversity and richness of this small island nation in the heart of the Mediterranean.

Malta is a nation of great historical importance. The traces of the Phoenicians, Romans, Arabs, Normans and other cultures can be found in their architecture, their language and their culture. The Knights of Malta, also known as the Order of Saint John, played an important role in the history of Europe, leaving a legacy that is still visible today in the capital, Valletta, and other places.

Maltese culture is characterized by its diversity and hospitality. Its festivals and customs, from carnival to religious celebrations, reflect the rich heritage of this island. The Maltese language, a mixture of Arabic, Italian and English, is a unique feature of Malta's identity.

Malta's unique geography, including its magnificent coastal landscapes, has made it a popular tourist destination. Wildlife, from Malta falcons to sea turtles, is of great importance for conservation. Maltese cuisine, from pastizzi to rabbit stew, offers culinary delights for all tastes.

Malta under British rule and its subsequent independence in 1964 are important chapters in the country's history. The post-war period brought modernisation and economic diversification, making Malta a thriving centre for financial services and tourism.

Valletta, the capital of Malta and a UNESCO World Heritage Site, impresses with its historic architecture and cultural richness. The three historic towns of Birgu, Senglea and Bormla are other treasures of the past that are still admired today.

The megalithic temples of Ħaġar Qim and Mnajdra bear witness to Malta's fascinating prehistoric past. The sister island of Gozo and the small island of Comino offer additional opportunities for exploration and relaxation.

The Blue Grotto, a natural wonder point, is a must-see for visitors who want to experience the beauty of the Maltese coast. The fortified city of Mdina, the quiet heart of Malta, enchants with its narrow streets and history.

The Maltese folk festivals and celebrations are an expression of the residents' joie de vivre and sense of community. The carnival in Malta has a long tradition and inspires with colorful costumes and parades.

The Maltese music scene ranges from traditional Għana to modern pop music. The art scene ranges from Caravaggio to contemporary art.

Religion plays an important role in Malta, from Roman times to the present day. The folklore and customs are alive and are celebrated at numerous festivals and events.

The craft and art of filigree are an important part of Maltese culture and identity. The Maltese language, unique in its kind, is a key to understanding this nation.

The school system and education in Malta are continuously evolving to meet the demands of the modern world. Medical care on the island is at a high level.

The Maltese legal system and judiciary ensure the rule of law and justice. Malta's economy is diverse, from tourism to the financial industry.

Maltese architecture tells a story that spans centuries. Malta's transport system is constantly being improved to meet the needs of the population and visitors.

Outdoor activities, such as diving and hiking, are a treat in the Maltese natural setting. The Maltese Carnival is a colourful spectacle that attracts thousands of visitors every year.

The nightlife in Malta offers a variety of bars, clubs and events for entertainment and pleasure. Maltese souvenirs and shopping offer memorabilia and local produce.

Naturalization in Malta allows people from different parts of the world to live on the island and become part of the community. The Maltese hospitality and culture of hospitality warmly welcome guests.

Sustainability and environmental protection are important concerns of Malta in order to protect the unique nature and environment. Malta's future is marked by opportunities and challenges, from the continuation of sustainability efforts to the further development of the economy and society.

With this final word, our journey through Malta, an island of historical importance and natural beauty, ends. May this book help to deepen understanding and appreciation of this fascinating country.

www.ingramcontent.com/pod-product-compliance
Lightning Source LLC
LaVergne TN
LVHW010032101125
825360LV00008B/300